FINDING YOUR TREASURE

A Monastic Journey through Lent

The Benedictine Monks
of Münsterschwarzach Abbey

Paulist Press
New York / Mahwah, NJ

Cover image by Darryl Brooks / Shutterstock.com
Cover design by Dawn Massa, Lightly Salted Graphics
Book design by Sharyn Banks

Originally published in German as *Unterwegs zu mir selbst* Copyright © 2018 Vier-Tuerme GmbH, Verlag, 97359 Münsterschwarzach Abtei; English translation by Peter Dahm Robertson, Copyright © 2020 by Paulist Press.

Library of Congress Cataloging-in-Publication Data

Names: Abtei Münsterschwarzach.
Title: Finding your treasure : a monastic journey through Lent / The Benedictine Monks of Münsterschwarzach Abbey.
Other titles: Unterwegs zu mir selbst. English
Description: New York : Paulist Press, [2020] | "Originally published in German as Unterwegs zu mir selbst copyright © 2018 Vier-Tuerme GmbH, Verlag, 97359 Münsterschwarzach Abtei; English translation-by Peter Dahm Robertson"—Title verso.
Identifiers: LCCN 2019005041 (print) | LCCN 2019017626 (ebook) | ISBN 9781587688515 (ebook) | ISBN 9780809154593 (pbk. : alk. paper)
Subjects: LCSH: Lent—Prayers and devotions.
Classification: LCC BX2170.L4 (ebook) | LCC BX2170.L4 A2813 2019 (print) | DDC 242/.34—dc23
LC record available at https://lccn.loc.gov/2019005041

ISBN 978-0-8091-5459-3 (paperback)
ISBN 978-1-58768-851-5 (e-book)

Published by Paulist Press
997 Macarthur Boulevard
Mahwah, New Jersey 07430
www.paulistpress.com

Printed and bound in the United States of America

Contents

Contents

Contents

Contents

Contents

Contents

Preface

The path into yourself, into your own center, is rarely straightforward and often full of surprises. Those who set out on the journey discover new insights, and perhaps wisdom they thought they had forgotten. Or answers to questions such as: What do I truly want? What supports me? What do I need for my life to succeed? But there is also plenty of steep terrain and darkness that needs to be navigated. One thing, however, is certain: only those who set out will ever arrive. And we may travel in the certainty that God is with us every step of the way. He is waiting for us. We can find God, if we are at home in ourselves.

THE MONKS OF MÜNSTERSCHWARZACH ABBEY WISH YOU A BLESSED JOURNEY THROUGH LENT!

SETTING
OUT

ASH WEDNESDAY

The journey

God is a God of journey. He journeyed for forty
years with his own people of Israel, from Egyptian
bondage into the freedom of the promised land.
Jesus, too, goes up to people and asks them to
"follow him"—literally, to go behind or after him.
This means starting out toward my own freedom,
opening myself up to that journey—breaking open
everything in me that has become hardened,
stubborn, and unyielding. That way, I can reconnect
with the feeling that God lives within me. I can
reconnect with the fact that I am a unique
expression of God.

—FATHER ZACHARIAS HEYES

THURSDAY AFTER ASH WEDNESDAY

Not just playing a role

When I was younger, there was a popular song we used to sing:

> Stop letting others choose
> The role you're gonna play,
> Or you'll be wearing masks
> Until your dying day.

All of us play many different roles every day—the role of a mother, father, partner, colleague, and so on. All these roles come with expectations. These forty days of Lent invite us to set out on a journey to find ourselves, to question our roles and the ways we live them. In what roles am I just functioning, and in what roles can I see myself? What roles do I really fulfill? I am more than just the person I think I ought to be in the eyes of others.

—FATHER ZACHARIAS HEYES

FRIDAY AFTER ASH WEDNESDAY

Listening inward

Years ago, one of my fellow monks told me, "God's voice is ever the quieter one." On Mount Horeb, the prophet Elijah encounters God in the sound of "sheer silence" (1 Kgs 19:12). God does not impose himself. He wants to be listened for. When all the noise and loud, external voices fall away, I can listen into myself and get in touch with my deepest inner being. This truest self is—since I am made in the image of God—God's being within me. When I feel that in the silence of my heart, I am "at one" with myself—that is where I find God resonating in me.

—FATHER ZACHARIAS HEYES

SATURDAY AFTER ASH WEDNESDAY

Leaving it out

One summer, I was a spiritual counselor for a sculpture course on the theme of "simplicity." By working on a block of stone, the artists reduce it. In order to transform the block into a figure, material must be chipped off, removed. The block of marble gains a clear shape, a clear expression and form, only when pieces of stone are taken away. What in my life do I need to leave out, chip away, shake off, reduce, omit in order to reach my truest self and cultivate a clearer, more structured, decisive profile?

—FATHER ZACHARIAS HEYES

LOOKING BACK

FIRST SUNDAY OF LENT

My origins

When I think back to the beginnings of my life—
even before I was born—out of millions of my
father's sperm cells, just one fused with my mother's
egg. Those very cells turned into me, and if a
different sperm cell had been faster, I would be a
different person today.

Is that random chance? Is it luck? Or was it
caused by someone, affirmed even?

Someone wanted me to be exactly the person I
am. Someone wanted me to have exactly those
genes I have today. Someone wanted that me to
become a person.

—ABBOT MICHAEL REEPEN

MONDAY OF THE FIRST WEEK OF LENT

A good start

What is my earliest memory? Standing up in my crib and seeing my mother come toward me? Or is it of playing with others in the sandbox or in preschool?

My earliest memories are of the people around me, those who fed and nursed me, my parents, siblings, grandparents—the people who walked with me in my first faltering steps through this world, who told me about God's goodness so early in my life. It is because I have experienced goodness that I can believe in goodness.

—ABBOT MICHAEL REEPEN

TUESDAY OF THE FIRST WEEK OF LENT

Imperfect, but supported

There is no ideal home. There aren't any ideal parents, ideal teachers or educators, just like there isn't an ideal monk or abbot.

Plenty goes wrong in any upbringing: not everything was perfect, and neither am I a perfect person, nor do I do things in the best possible way. If we think we need to do it all by ourselves, we're overwhelmed immediately. How helpful it is to believe that there is someone else who holds his protective hand over my imperfect life and works.

—ABBOT MICHAEL REEPEN

WEDNESDAY OF THE FIRST WEEK OF LENT

Making peace

If I want to, I can choose to spend a lifetime suffering from, complaining about, or sighing over all the things that went wrong or were unfair in my childhood, youth, and through the rest of my life. Some people are constantly brooding over all those things—and it changes nothing.

Thank God that I have grown up: I am above the past now. I am no longer the young, defenseless person I once was. I can take my life in my own hands and change it. Making peace with the past—or refusing to—is my choice. That doesn't erase the hurt, but it does give me the space to heal.

—ABBOT MICHAEL REEPEN

THURSDAY OF THE FIRST WEEK OF LENT

Trust

How lucky I've been! I've witnessed so much good, so much talent and ability! I have been blessed to discover so many things, and to develop so many gifts—not least because there were people close to me who trusted me and encouraged me: You can do it! You'll make it!

And I tried, and made it, and learned, and realized: I can do it, and it gives me joy. I am discovering something new about myself—what a blessing!

—ABBOT MICHAEL REEPEN

FRIDAY OF THE FIRST WEEK OF LENT

Staying on track

Time and time again, life pushed me into tight corners. A crisis loomed, and I wanted to run away, avoid it, sidestep the situation. And from somewhere, there came the voice: Don't run away! Face up to the crisis! Navigate through that tight corner! Stay with it, keep on it, and keep going— and I emerged as a different person. Sometimes it hurt: I suffer and weep, but I stay the course. And then everything is transformed. There's a light at the end of the tunnel. My heart opens wide, joy comes back, and I keep walking my own path.

—ABBOT MICHAEL REEPEN

SATURDAY OF THE FIRST WEEK OF LENT

Saved

I've felt it again and again, even as a child: It comes out of the blue, all of a sudden in everyday moments, at work, during breaks, on bike rides, visiting with friends, or alone in my armchair. I am caught up in something and know myself safe and supported, touched by love, shaken by presence, seized with joy. And then I know: I am saved!

I can't get there on my own. I can't force it. All I can do is be ready.

—ABBOT MICHAEL REEPEN

SEEING THE SHADOW

SECOND SUNDAY OF LENT

Self-acceptance

True self-acceptance means coming to terms with my Shadow. According to C. G. Jung, our Shadow consists of those parts of us we do not allow ourselves to see because they do not correspond to the image we wish to have of ourselves. These aspects are banished into the Shadow. There, however, they live on, until a repressed emotion may express itself, for example, as sentimentality. Or if we have repressed aggression because it does not correspond to our image of ourselves, it may express itself in coldness or sternness—or in depression, if we direct the aggression toward ourselves. By the time we reach middle age, at the latest, we are challenged to confront our Shadow and reconcile with it, or else we become inwardly torn, leading to illness.

—FATHER ANSELM GRÜN

MONDAY OF THE SECOND WEEK OF LENT

Humility

A person who does not confront their own Shadow unconsciously projects their Shadow onto others. Instead of admitting their own lack of discipline, for example, that trait is identified only in others—in a spouse, friend, or colleague who does not live their life consistently and lets themselves go too much.

Accepting our Shadow does not mean simply living out that part of ourselves. Instead, it involves acknowledging it to ourselves. That requires humility, the courage to step down from our lofty ideal and lower ourselves into the dirt of our own reality. The word *humility*, in fact, comes from the Latin root *humus*, meaning "earth"—we must accept our own earthly nature.

—FATHER ANSELM GRÜN

TUESDAY OF THE SECOND WEEK OF LENT

Seeking the treasure

Jesus shows us the path of humility: the path deep
into ourselves, into our own depth. There we
encounter our own Shadow and the earthliness of
our lives—and all our old wounds. It is here and
only here that we can find our greatest treasure,
that precious pearl: our own true self. Some people
feel as though they only ever dig through the dirt
of their own life's field: their hands grow dirty,
but they never find anything. All the while,
however, they are close to their treasure. They
should keep digging, trusting in God. Someday,
the treasure will be revealed in the soil of our soul.

—FATHER ANSELM GRÜN

WEDNESDAY OF THE SECOND WEEK OF LENT

Trusting in the good

We want to be good—but then we discover our capacity for evil. We want to be loving—but then we discover the hate and vengefulness we bear, as well. We are afraid of these weeds and want to pull them up. But if we do this, we also pull up the wheat (see Matt 13:29–30). The weed Jesus is referring to in this image is ryegrass—which looks like wheat and has roots that are often entangled with those of wheat.

Anyone who, out of a love of perfection, wants to pull up all the weeds out of the soil of the soul would also never harvest any wheat. Their life would be fruitless. A fruitful life is never an expression of absolute perfection or infallibility. Instead, it comes from trusting that the wheat is stronger than the weeds, and that the weeds can be separated out during harvest.

—FATHER ANSELM GRÜN

THURSDAY OF THE SECOND WEEK OF LENT

Bearing the cross

We should take up our own cross. The cross unifies all contradictions. In the same way, we should accept all our self-contradiction, including our Shadow, which darkens our idealized image of our self. Taking up our cross means saying yes to all the things that cross us; saying yes to the suffering we feel, to our failures, to failed relationships and the fractures in our life story.

Only if we reconcile ourselves to the cross life places upon us can we pray without distraction. True prayer requires unconditional self-acceptance. Otherwise, we are perpetually interrupted and distracted by the things we are rebelling against inwardly.

—FATHER ANSELM GRÜN

FRIDAY OF THE SECOND WEEK OF LENT

It is well

Sometimes, when a person comes to me who is suffering from their Shadow, from the circumstances of their life, I give them an exercise. I tell them to sit before an icon and say, looking at the image of Christ, "It is well. Everything is meant to be like this, and it is good that it is like this. I thank you that I am the person I am today. I thank you for my personal history, for the highs and lows, dead ends and detours in my life." Often, this isn't easy. If I've just encountered darkness, I may resist being grateful for it. But if I try to look at my life and my character from the point of view of God, and if I thank God, then I will feel a deep peace arise within me. I feel peace, and I can sense that truly all is well, that the things in my life that are hard are the very things that keep me alert, so that I can trust in God and not in myself.

—FATHER ANSELM GRÜN

SATURDAY OF THE SECOND WEEK OF LENT

Greater than our hearts

It is even more difficult to reconcile ourselves with our own failings and forgive ourselves for them. We can only forgive ourselves, however, if we believe with all our heart that God has forgiven us; that we are accepted by God unconditionally. Many do not take God's forgiveness seriously. They may say they believe in it, but in their heart of hearts, they have not forgiven themselves for their failures. They still reproach themselves for the guilt they have heaped upon themselves. Within them, they have a merciless judge who is harsh in his verdicts.

God is much more forgiving of us than we are of ourselves. Even if our hearts condemn us: "God is greater than our hearts, and he knows everything" (1 John 3:20).

—FATHER ANSELM GRÜN

DISCOVERING
THE TREASURE

THIRD SUNDAY OF LENT

My individual gifts

Just like every other human being, I am personally accepted and affirmed by God as his child. God created the world and became man in Christ, and those acts are the very foundation of his affirmation and love for me. God has given me special dignity that no one can take from me. And God has given me all the things that make me special: my being, my soul, my body with all my individual gifts.

What are these gifts that God has given me? What do I find difficult right now? What am I proud of? What do I feel grateful for?

—FATHER CHRISTOPH GERHARD

MONDAY OF THE THIRD WEEK OF LENT

Unimaginable potential

The talents I have been given are not limited to the things I do well—the areas where I am supposedly better than others. Often, it's the hidden qualities, the buried treasure, that determine who I am. Often, it's my quiet and more unassuming side that hides unimaginable potential.

What in me longs to be developed further? Is there a hidden side to me that I could live out more? What are the gifts in my life that I want to keep unfolding?

—FATHER CHRISTOPH GERHARD

TUESDAY OF THE THIRD WEEK OF LENT

Shouldering responsibility

Our abilities and strengths are sometimes called our "gifts"—and that is exactly right. All my feeling and thinking give me the ability to do good for others. This makes me responsible for the things that can happen in this world through me. What I do and perceive in this world turn out to be my very own choice—and that choice is my answer to God's yes to my life.

What things do I want to take more and deeper responsibility for? Which part of my life needs special attention right now? Are there persons or areas entrusted specifically to me and my gifts?

—FATHER CHRISTOPH GERHARD

WEDNESDAY OF THE THIRD WEEK OF LENT

Letting my light shine

When I feel secure, it's often easy to let my light shine. It feels natural and joyful and confirms that I am bringing my best into the world. Others can live through and with me, and I take part in what others offer me.

But there are also moments in which I need more courage. To look and listen when people are suffering—and to stand up for them. To speak up against injustice. To do what is necessary, every single day.

—FATHER CHRISTOPH GERHARD

THURSDAY OF THE THIRD WEEK OF LENT

Giving myself to others

God gave me my talents so that I can live and use them—for myself, for others, and for the kingdom of God. In the parable of the talents, the master praises those slaves who return double what they were given. In the same way, our life longs to be enlarged and fulfilled.

God rejoices when we pass on the gifts of our life. If I use my gifts well, I can witness firsthand the miracle that by giving away my gifts, my life isn't cheapened but enriched: it becomes deeper, more beautiful, and is fulfilled.

—FATHER CHRISTOPH GERHARD

FRIDAY OF THE THIRD WEEK OF LENT

The courage to serve

Humility is sometimes described as "the courage to serve"—the bravery to use one's abilities to the benefit of others, rather than letting one's gifts go unused. Such bravery requires accepting one's truth as it is, including those moments in which others' abilities apparently exceed our own, or those moments in which I am insecure. Humility also means reconciling with one's Shadow as well as with one's gifts, and using both to the benefit of others. All our abilities are gifts that have been given to us—and to the world around us.

—FATHER CHRISTOPH GERHARD

SATURDAY OF THE THIRD WEEK OF LENT

Following your inner treasure map

In order to find or rediscover a hidden treasure, you need a treasure map. But treasure maps aren't always as reliable or precise as we might want them to be. In those moments, we need sensitivity and patience in the face of life's imprecision. We can find and tap into previously unimagined potential and strength if we wholeheartedly follow our lust for life. Only then can we unearth the treasure—the gift for ourselves and for others.

Let's trust our inner voices; trust in the Holy Spirit to show us the path to life.

—FATHER CHRISTOPH GERHARD

SOURCES OF STRENGTH

FOURTH SUNDAY OF LENT

Sources of strength

Each of us has tasted a dark brown square of the kind of temptation that melts in your mouth. Just one bite of sugary sweetness—not a bad thing during the day, right? But chocolate is only one of the temptations that continuously cross my path. Whatever our age or maturity, temptation remains a constant theme throughout our lives.

These days, we have many different offers and options to choose from. We lack nothing. That's great, but the danger is that we can't feel what it is that we really need. What is my soul thirsting for? What is my deepest longing?

—FATHER ISAAK GRÜNBERGER

MONDAY OF THE FOURTH WEEK OF LENT

Things that matter

Some evenings, I catch myself thinking, "That's it? That's all today was?" Whenever that happens, I know that I have once again spent a day just "doing my chores." I didn't take the time to look at a flower by the wayside, watch children at play, or lie in a hammock thinking about everything and nothing, guilt free. Everyday life often leaves no room even for an honest "How are you?," an encouraging word, a hospital visit, a healing conversation after a fight. So it is good to remind ourselves that life is more than what we are assigned from outside ourselves.

—FATHER ISAAK GRÜNBERGER

TUESDAY OF THE FOURTH WEEK OF LENT

Being good to yourself

Lent is a time to be good to oneself, to care for oneself. That isn't egotism, quite the opposite: caring for myself is the basis of a good life that can be a blessing to others. However intractable a situation seems, it's always easier to find a solution if I look at myself and my inadequacies with an eye of loving-kindness. God looks at us kindly and with love—why shouldn't we do the same?

—FATHER ISAAK GRÜNBERGER

WEDNESDAY OF THE FOURTH WEEK OF LENT

With open eyes

To me, nature is God's love made tangible. His providence is visible everywhere we look. And yet, too often we rush from one place to another without pausing even for a moment, without daring to glance at the streets of our city, the countryside around us. Walking through nature with open eyes can give us strength and lighten our heart. By walking through nature with open eyes, I can discover the beauty and wonder inherent in creation. It's easy. I just need to open my eyes.

—FATHER ISAAK GRÜNBERGER

THURSDAY OF THE FOURTH WEEK OF LENT

Mutual support

My achievements on their own can never make me happy. I don't need to push myself constantly as if I must do everything alone. I live with others, and I live because of others: we are all connected and dependent on one another. They live through me, too. We all support one another. Our mutual gratitude supports us. So when someone thanks me, there's no need to be coy: "Oh, don't worry about it, it was nothing." When others thank me and when I am able to thank others, we are expressing the thanks we give to our Creator for making us so valued by one another.

—FATHER ISAAK GRÜNBERGER

FRIDAY OF THE FOURTH WEEK OF LENT

The right word

Sometimes, I can't find the right word for what goes on in our world. It seems that I am at a loss for words. They may have been too big for me. Now, I hold with the little words, put them on like shoes and walk around in them. Words like *hope*, *honesty*, *courage*, *mindfulness*, *clarity*, *intuition*, *responsibility*, *freedom*, *trust*, *love*, and *strength*.

Do you know moments like that, in which you lose all your trust in yourself, and then suddenly have courage, hope, strength again? The source from which a person draws courage, and the way in which that person draws courage—those two things show what a person thinks of reality and of God's power. To me, these little and yet sometimes too big words are what give me strength. Sometimes the right word speaks to me, this one word that comes to me and is just right in that one moment. The word of encouragement.

—FATHER ISAAK GRÜNBERGER

SATURDAY OF THE FOURTH WEEK OF LENT

Above all

"I don't believe in God, but I miss him." I am touched by this sentence, written by the English novelist Julian Barnes. If someone, who calls himself an atheist, does not believe in God, then why does he miss him? Perhaps Barnes has a sense that God might be someone who would do him good.

For me, God is a reality. Faith in him makes my life richer; my life becomes meaningful through my relationship with God. Why? It's good to know that there is a power that gives me a gift that neither I can give myself nor all the world can give me.

—FATHER ISAAK GRÜNBERGER

FREEDOM

FIFTH SUNDAY OF LENT

Freedom in the world

Some things are needed to live: air, food, environment, neighborhood. And so I am tied to the world around me.

If I accept this bond, I can move freely within it.

I live freely in thinking, feeling, doing and not doing.

If I am responsible for my freedom in the world around me—if I respond to the world— I remain free within these bounds.

—FATHER MEINRAD DUFNER

MONDAY OF THE FIFTH WEEK OF LENT

Two kinds of dependence

As a child, depending on my parents kept me alive. As a growing man, my growth depended on fighting that dependence. As an adult, I must distinguish: Where does dependence give me life? Where does dependence stifle my life?

Today: Saying yes to the dependence that gives me life. Refusing where it deadens me.

—FATHER MEINRAD DUFNER

TUESDAY OF THE FIFTH WEEK OF LENT

Me and you

I am me! You are you! So, affirm differences, find commonalities, let the past be past, leave the future open. Take the present in our own hands, together.

Today: Saying what I always wanted to say. But with kindness.

—FATHER MEINRAD DUFNER

WEDNESDAY OF THE FIFTH WEEK OF LENT

Expectations

Not to expect too much of myself.
Not to expect too much of others.
Not to expect too much of life.
Not to expect too much of God.
But to walk with trust the path before me.
In that way, what is expected will find me.

Today: Encountering each and everyone with trust and hope.

—FATHER MEINRAD DUFNER

THURSDAY OF THE FIFTH WEEK OF LENT

Yes and no

Think "No,"
     say "No,"
     feel "No,"
so that "Yes"
can be resurrected,
simple and pure.

Today: Saying no with courage, so I can say yes
with conviction.

—FATHER MEINRAD DUFNER

FRIDAY OF THE FIFTH WEEK OF LENT

Giving my self

Listening to my body, soul, feelings,
    thoughts, hopes.
Not going along just to get along!
Contributing more, trusting more, involving
    myself with all my creativity and
    individuality.

Today: Showing more of my self. And just like that,
I am a greater part of others' lives.

—FATHER MEINRAD DUFNER

SATURDAY OF THE FIFTH WEEK OF LENT

It is what it is

> Some things "just are": a talent or a
>   handicap, a demand, fate.
> I can move through these freely.
> They are merely proof that I am alive, am
>   unique, have a meaning and purpose
>   that can only be revealed to me in my
>   acceptance.

Today: Stilling my faculty of judgment. Quieting
my contrariness. "It is what it is, says love"
(Erich Fried).

—FATHER MEINRAD DUFNER

FINDING THE CENTER

PALM SUNDAY

At home in God—and in myself

Sometimes we say of a person, "He's not centered. She's not at home in herself." When I am centered, I become calm. I am not as shaken when someone hurts me.

On Palm Sunday, Jesus shows us how to stay centered, both during his supporters' jubilation and throughout his adversaries' attacks. He refuses to be provoked by insults. He retreats into his center. There he is protected, supported, at home in himself, with God. During Holy Week, we can learn from Jesus how to be centered in ourselves despite the turbulent events around us.

—FATHER ANSELM GRÜN

MONDAY OF HOLY WEEK

The path into our center

Many people long to feel at home in themselves. But they have trouble finding a path toward their own center. The path into our center runs through our emotions and passions, right through the chaos of our feelings.

Jesus speaks of a treasure buried in a field. The treasure refers to our truest self, our inner center. But in order to reach it, we need to get our hands dirty: we must dig through our jealousy and envy, through our anger and frustration, through fear and depression. We cannot reach the center except through truth. If we have the courage to dig down into the dirt and the chaos within us, we can reach our center. We can arrive at our truest self.

—FATHER ANSELM GRÜN

TUESDAY OF HOLY WEEK

Our uniqueness

According to the medieval theologian Thomas Aquinas, each person is a unique expression of God. Our task is to reveal this unique expression to the world. We recognize this expression of God in ourselves when we grow quiet and feel deeply into our soul. When I feel in harmony with myself, when I feel at home in myself—in those moments, I can trust that I am in touch with the unique way God has expressed himself in me. That is when my life falls into place and becomes a blessing to others.

—FATHER ANSELM GRÜN

WEDNESDAY OF HOLY WEEK

Pure freedom

A person who lives what is within them is authentic. An authentic person is simply there and feels no need to justify themselves or prove something to others. Jesus lived this for us in his Passion. He was simply there. He did not defend himself. And yet no one could ignore or deny his aura. Every person sensed that here is someone who is completely real, completely natural. He is not living out ideas others have projected onto him. He is simply there. This is a thing I long for: simply to be, without a thought as to the purpose. That is pure freedom.

—FATHER ANSELM GRÜN

HOLY THURSDAY

Broken open

On Holy Thursday, Jesus washes the dust off his disciples' feet, touching their calluses and wounds. He takes each disciple's Achilles' heel in his hands to show them the path to their truest self.

The path to our center leads through our wounds. The wounds shatter my mask, break open the shell I surround myself with in order to protect myself from being hurt by others. I am broken open so that I can touch my truest self, can dare to set out into the love of my fellow brothers and sisters.

—FATHER ANSELM GRÜN

GOOD FRIDAY

Making peace

On Good Friday, we venerate the cross of Jesus Christ. This cross bridges all contradictions and opposites: heaven and earth, light and dark, man and woman, the conscious and the subconscious. If a person wants to become whole—at least according to C. G. Jung—their path must go via the cross.

Accepting the cross, bearing one's cross, means accepting oneself with all one's contradictions: with one's love and aggression, with one's faith and nonbelief, with one's trust and fear. In this way, the cross can become a tool for making peace with ourselves and with the people around us.

—FATHER ANSELM GRÜN

HOLY SATURDAY

Burying the past

On Holy Saturday, we look on the grave of Jesus. The buried Jesus invites us to bury all that keeps us from living the unique expression of God that is within us. He invites us to bury old grievances that cut us off from those around us; to bury old ways of life that hold us back, such as the tendency to hide our light under a bushel, or to make things all about us. Meditating on Jesus in the grave, we can think of many things we might want to bury, so that on Easter, we too can be resurrected into a new, authentic life of freedom.

—FATHER ANSELM GRÜN

EASTER SUNDAY

The eternal wellspring

We celebrate Easter so that the life of the resurrected Christ may rise up in us as well; so that the resurrection of Jesus may break open everything in us that has become rigid and unyielding; so that the angel may roll away the stone blocking our path. We celebrate Easter so that the eternal life of the resurrected Christ may permeate everything within us, leading us into the abundance of life that Jesus promised: "I came that they may have life, and have it abundantly" (John 10:10). Abundance means that our deepest longing for life, love, and freedom is fulfilled—that we live out of a boundless source, a wellspring that never runs dry because it is Godly.

—FATHER ANSELM GRÜN

About the Authors

THE BENEDICTINE MONKS OF MÜNSTERSCHWARZACH ABBEY

Abbot Michael Reepen was born in 1959 and has been the abbot at Münsterschwarzach Abbey since May 2006. After returning from a missionary period in Tanzania, he served as Master of novices, overseeing the spiritual orientation of the new monks of the community. He additionally leads courses at the Münsterschwarzach guesthouse.

Father Meinrad Dufner was born in 1946 and is a priest, author, painter, and visual artist. He studied philosophy and theology in St. Ottilien, Bonn, and Würzburg. From 1982 to 1994, he served as Master of novices, overseeing the spiritual orientation of the new monks of the community. While always artistically active, since 1991 he has also been a crisis counselor at Recollectio house, an institution of the Münsterschwarzach Abbey.

Father Christoph Gerhard was born in 1964. He is the cellarer and finance manager of the

Münsterschwarzach Abbey. He has been practicing the monastic science of astronomy for twenty years, with a focus on spotting deep sky objects from the monastery's own observatory. For Christoph Gerhard, astronomy is connected to faith and a lived spirituality of creation. For more information on astronomy in the monastery, see http://www.klostersternwarte.de/.

Father Anselm Grün was born in 1945. He is one of the most widely read Christian authors of today, reaching an audience across all denominations and nationalities. Dom Anselm has written over 380 books, which have been translated into 34 languages and have sold around 15 million copies to date. His spiritual guidance and counsel, regardless of religious denomination, have made him one of Germany's best-known authors on spirituality. For more information, see https://www.anselm-gruen.de/.

Father Isaak Grünberger was born in 1964 and was the superior at St. Benedict Monastery in Würzburg from 2002 to 2010. Since 2017, he has served as a priest in the parish community of St. Benedikt.

Father Zacharias Heyes was born in 1971. After studying theology and working as a missionary providing developmental aid in East Africa, he now serves as a crisis counselor at Recollectio house, an institution of the Münsterschwarzach Abbey, for priests, religious, and ecclesiastical staff members who need to resolve their crisis. He additionally leads numerous courses and workshops on various themes, such as stone sculpture, at the Münsterschwarzach guesthouse.